This book was born when three friends had the same realization at the same time on the same night. The realization was hysterically simple. They realized that they were *"alive."* And then they realized, *"holy shit,"* that's pretty amazing.

Now we, the authors, can imagine you, the reader, sitting there reading that last sentence and silently mouthing "Duh" to yourself. But before you mouth anything, we'd just ask that you take a second and query yourself the following:

How much of your day is spent living in the base-line awareness that your very existence is a friggin' miracle? The reason I ask is because if I had to wager, I'd say it's not nearly as much as the time you spent wishing your job was more fulfilling, that your parents were less annoying, that your partner was nicer, or that your kids were easier, the weather was better, your bank account was fatter, that you were skinnier, the list goes on and on....

If you get depressed thinking about that, take heart. You're not alone. Most of us do this.

We humans go through life with this sort of low-level hum of dissatisfaction. It's a big part of what makes us, us. In fact, it's this drive to change our circumstances, to improve, to hack our conditions, that has helped us grow from small bands of hunter gatherers to larger agricultural societies to the enormous, interdependent information-based mega-cities of today.

Yet all this thinking and emoting and striving and doing and struggling has come at a terrible cost. We've lost the ability to do one very essential thing, which is honor the "holy-shit-ness" of our of daily existence.

Why?

Perhaps because this precious gift called consciousness is so seamless and glitch-free that for most of our lives we feel like it's not enough. It's almost too vanilla. So what do we do?

We pile thoughts, memories, resentments, hopes, expectations over it like toppings at an ice cream sundae bar, until the bare miraculous fact of this "I am-ness" is completely covered.

It is our hope that this book can be a fun, thought-provoking, sense-stimulating way to strip off all the crap we put on our perfect scoops of consciousness ice-cream so that we can all live in the joyous reality of the one thing we should never, ever forget.

Holy Shit, We're Alive.

P.S. - Feel free to explore your creativity, sharing feelings and moments of gratitude on the following pages. In this space, all things are possible. Please pass it on.

Holy shit, we're alive.

Holy shit, we're alive.

Holy shit, we're alive.

Holy shit, we're alive.

Holy shit, we're alive.

Holy shit, we're alive.

Holy shit, we're alive.

Holy shit, we're alive.

Holy shit, we're alive.

Holy shit, we're alive.

Holy shit, we're alive.

Holy shit, we're alive.

Holy shit, we're alive.

Holy shit, we're alive.

Holy shit, we're alive.

Holy shit, we're alive.

Holy shit, we're alive.

Holy shit, we're alive.

Holy shit, we're alive.

Holy shit, we're alive.

Holy shit, we're alive.

Holy shit, we're alive.

Holy shit, we're alive.

Holy shit, we're alive.

Holy shit, we're alive.

Holy shit, we're alive.

Holy shit, we're alive.

Holy shit, we're alive.

Holy shit, we're alive.

Holy shit, we're alive.

Holy shit, we're alive.

Holy shit, we're alive.

Holy shit, we're alive.

Holy shit, we're alive.

Holy shit, we're alive.

Holy shit, we're alive.

Holy shit, we're alive.

Holy shit, we're alive.

Holy shit, we're alive.

Holy shit, we're alive.

Holy shit, we're alive.

Holy shit, we're alive.

Holy shit, we're alive.

Holy shit, we're alive.

Holy shit, we're alive.

Holy shit, we're alive.

Holy shit, we're alive.

Holy shit, we're alive.

Holy shit, we're alive.

Holy shit, we're alive.

Holy shit, we're alive.

Holy shit, we're alive.

Holy shit, we're alive.

Holy shit, we're alive.

Holy shit, we're alive.

Holy shit, we're alive.

Holy shit, we're alive.

Holy shit, we're alive.

Holy shit, we're alive.

Holy shit, we're alive.

Holy shit, we're alive.

Holy shit, we're alive.

Holy shit, we're alive.

Holy shit, we're alive.

Holy shit, we're alive.

Holy shit, we're alive.

Holy shit, we're alive.

Holy shit, we're alive.

Holy shit, we're alive.

Holy shit, we're alive.

Holy shit, we're alive.

Holy shit, we're alive.

Holy shit, we're alive.

Holy shit, we're alive.

Holy shit, we're alive.

Holy shit, we're alive.

Holy shit, we're alive.

Holy shit, we're alive.

Holy shit, we're alive.

Holy shit, we're alive.

Holy shit, we're alive.

Holy shit, we're alive.

Holy shit, we're alive.

Holy shit, we're alive.

Holy shit, we're alive.

Holy shit, we're alive.

Holy shit, we're alive.

Holy shit, we're alive.

Holy shit, we're alive.

Holy shit, we're alive.

Holy shit, we're alive.

Holy shit, we're alive.

Holy shit, we're alive.

Holy shit, we're alive.

Holy shit, we're alive.

Holy shit, we're alive.

Holy shit, we're alive.

Holy shit, we're alive.

Holy shit, we're alive.

Holy shit, we're alive.

Holy shit, we're alive.

Holy shit, we're alive.

Holy shit, we're alive.

Holy shit, we're alive.

Holy shit, we're alive.

Holy shit, we're alive.

Holy shit, we're alive.

Holy shit, we're alive.

Holy shit, we're alive.

Holy shit, we're alive.

Holy shit, we're alive.

Holy shit, we're alive.

Holy shit, we're alive.

Holy shit, we're alive.

Holy shit, we're alive.

Holy shit, we're alive.

Holy shit, we're alive.

Holy shit, we're alive.

Holy shit, we're alive.

Holy shit, we're alive.

Holy shit, we're alive.

Holy shit, we're alive.

Holy shit, we're alive.

Holy shit, we're alive.

Holy shit, we're alive.

Holy shit, we're alive.

Holy shit, we're alive.

Holy shit, we're alive.

Holy shit, we're alive.

Holy shit, we're alive.

Holy shit, we're alive.

Holy shit, we're alive.

Holy shit, we're alive.

Holy shit, we're alive.

Holy shit, we're alive.

Holy shit, we're alive.

Holy shit, we're alive.

Holy shit, we're alive.

Holy shit, we're alive.

Holy shit, we're alive.

Holy shit, we're alive.

Holy shit, we're alive.

Holy shit, we're alive.

Holy shit, we're alive.

Holy shit, we're alive.

Holy shit, we're alive.

Holy shit, we're alive.

Holy shit, we're alive.

Holy shit, we're alive.

Holy shit, we're alive.

Holy shit, we're alive.

Holy shit, we're alive.

Holy shit, we're alive.

Holy shit, we're alive.

Holy shit, we're alive.

Holy shit, we're alive.

Holy shit, we're alive.

Holy shit, we're alive.

Holy shit, we're alive.

Holy shit, we're alive.

Holy shit, we're alive.

Holy shit, we're alive.

Holy shit, we're alive.

Holy shit, we're alive.

Holy shit, we're alive.

Holy shit, we're alive.

Holy shit, we're alive.

Holy shit, we're alive.

Holy shit, we're alive.

Holy shit, we're alive.

Holy shit, we're alive.

Holy shit, we're alive.

Holy shit, we're alive.

Holy shit, we're alive.

Holy shit...